Abyss

Kate Helou

Presentation by *BookLeaf Publishing*

Web: www.bookleafpub.com

E-mail: info@bookleafpub.com

ISBN: 9789357744904

First edition 2023

*For all of my English teachers throughout
the years from Greenleaf Elementary
School, Falcon Ridge Middle School,
Eastview High School, and my English
professors at the College of Saint Benedict
and St. John's University- Thank you for
pushing me to work hard at writing and for
inspiring my confidence as a developing
writer.*

ACKNOWLEDGEMENT

Thank you to Dr. Jessica Harkins and Dr. Christopher Bolin for giving me the tools to write and refine my work, as well as providing me with valuable feedback that has shaped the way that I write poetry.

And a special thank you to Izzy Bui, my friend who introduced me to BookLeaf Publishing.

Inhabitance

i. Space

Surrounded by empty ringing.
Exposed to tonal earth,
Floating in the absence of moon face.

Shiny, swirling grains mimic
Stars left behind,
Letters for the eternal tick
In my hands, the itch
Of my inferior ear.

ii. Body

Porous by design,
Dense left ribs.
Soft right ventricle.
What space do we inhabit?

The drift of leaves across my cheek,
The wiping away of salt;
A product of our metamorphosis.

Clarity of skin,
Speckled, vintage tortoise shell

Glasses on a dusty shelf.

iii. Self

The matching of our breath, like the soft socks
Next to my dresser drawer.
Touching your heart, tracing my finger down
To the queen of the deck.
Poke my eye, the center of your vertigo.

I'm right where you left me.
You're left behind.

Perception

Sea glass shining beneath
 The rolling thunder of waves
 Colors array in sunbeams pulling
 Light out of its subjects.
 Prisms dancing in a sphere
 Cut into me, forcing me to appear
 As myself to you, do my eyes ask the same of you?
 Or do they wander around the field,
 Blurred by judgement, honesty, or other beings?
 I am afraid of losing; one blink and the moment's gone
 Except in my head where it's endlessly replayed.
 Figure-eight glass shakes sand down
 The spiral of my timely core,
 Reminding me that once a grain passes
 From above to below, it's buried by its own kind.
 Wishing for more chances,
 Hoping for the finite nature of time to expire.
 The rubbing of two coins, the smudging of glass.
 When the purse breaks, the glass shatters.
 Shards into the sea and lost in my chest.

Sometimes, there is nothing I can see
Except your eyes boring into me.

Daisy

Throbbing despair ebbs in my blood
 The culmination of hope
Repeatedly grown then maimed
Not unlike a daisy gasping for breath
While drowning in sprinkles of
Rain that aim to soothe,
Yet smother.
Sinking in tears of demise,
Every ocean has a floor.
While inking words onto parchment,
Single droplets destroy the fine lines
Of commitment from pen to page.

Lies

Crinkled eyes,
 lop-sided smile,
and wisps of hair in every direction.

The outside shows
a fun-loving woman,
powerful, yet soft.

But unseen
and unheard,
lies untold

history.

The inside knows
a painful destruction
of body and mind.

Soul intertwined
with good-intentioned
others

truly believing
they know
what's best.

But through the comments,
the suggestions,
the unwarranted advice,

lies a brain.
Intelligent and full of life,
marred by genetics and chemically deficient.

She exists.

Just trying to survive.
And through it all,
lies a woman seeking to thrive.

Rose Petals

My lips should be rose petals but are instead
 Saltwater, remnants crystalized and then
 Swirled onto my tongue, dissolving as if they
were never there.
 All that remains are bitter buds resting there
without drink to
 Moisten them. Cracked yet closed,
 Sealed by the last bit of dew
 Trying to escape the eternal trap of discourse,
 Ruffling over the crevices of my brain and
slowly
 Finding their way back to my lips.

 The cure sits on my desk,
 Daring me to approach but never allowing
myself the
 Satisfaction of grasping it in my hands.
 Eyes glued to the tube that would cease the
 Parched state of the gate to my thoughts,
 I roll over in warmth.

Here I am safe, the only discomfort the
 Possibility of losing sanity as the last
 Condensation leaves my lips and therefore my
mind.

I linger in the folds of worn sheets, surrendering to the
 Power of sleep that drags me down under consciousness.

Labyrinth

A combination of intricate tracks;
Blood melded into bruises left by the caged
Animal that threatens to permeate our path.
Passages through the moss, red with our fever,
Burning moth wings beat against paper lanterns.
Refuge. How will you find me?
Sobs wracking me rigid: desperate. You
Are the lucid dream I lie awake with;
Even the promise of nightfall
Provides me no exit.

Out of Depths

An inner circle aspires to
 Illuminate a crib without its inhabitant.
 Bathed in light, faces unknown,
 The soft metal bars a precursor to
 The life provided, one can sink into stone
 Or fly with fire.
 Taut sheets a reminder of constraints
 Placed on little ones, carpet threadbare
 In the footsteps of lifetimes.
 Open windows swirl breezes, shifting embraces
 Until there is no warmth recovered from their
arms.
 Rippling curtains render his mind defied, yet
defined in choices
 That warp his body, spirit decoded.
 He emerges from the wall of flipped switches
 And smiles.

Abyss

Lost in rolling riches
 A rock curves up toward the light
 Casting down on a single mirror,
 Refracting bright white light
 Through the darkness of the deep.
 Each spot of light showcases her fantasies;
 She wishes to emerge triumphant from
 The shackles of the objects she has gathered.

 She has everything.
 But nothing she wants.
 Yet she gravitates toward all of it.
 No matter how shiny or faded,
 She thinks she wants it.

 Translucent sheens distort her things,
 Has she ever seen how they are supposed to
look?
 Or does she suppose they should appear this
way?

 When she reaches the top, she takes a breath
away
 From the constraints of everything below;
 Lungs mesmerized by the freedom of air.

Sinking back to the bottom,
She dreams of what could be
Never taking action to make it so.
She examines the metal, the glass, the wood,
All finding a new home on their rocky shelves,
Wishing she would find hers.

She would turn back the clock and do it
differently,
Except the clock before her doesn't tick
And the candle in front of her doesn't burn
And the camera near her doesn't capture
likenesses anymore.
She wishes to float toward the light.

Dissonance

Hot tea burns my tongue.
The dissonance of a chorus when
The melody's already been sung.
Ceramic tile shattered by the face of a hammer
Belonging to a guy.
Vibrant flowers ripped from the vine.
Bright white carpet
With a fresh stain of wine.
The smell of air after watercolor rain
Shriveled by the stench of car exhaust.
An old map with winding trails trying
Not to get lost.
A caged songbird that cannot fly.
The color of your words when
You lie.

Doing the Right Thing

Out of televisions
The woman in her red dress,
The man in his sport coat,
Dance around the kitchen never cooking,

-But unaware of watching pupils
Reflecting the soft glow of the screen-

He kisses her, she smiles
Twisting her pearls around a
Polished finger.

-Without tearing eyes away,
The couch is bathed in the glow
But is missing my other-

She calls to him,
Ringing the bell.
When did she make dinner?

-Empty takeout boxes sit
In the glow-

He sits at the kitchen table,

Napkin tied around his neck.
She tightens it, setting his plate down anyway.
He doesn't complain about the peas.

She asks about his day,
He answers.
They sit in silence, plates clean,
Feeling each other's presence.
They look at each other, making love.

-We are not them-

Signals of the Sacred

In the cold, worthless state
 Of my mind, blood runs
 Slow, but my heart beats fast,
 like a small plume of feathers whipping
 In the wind, but they never hurt.

In every beat of
Blood I find more pain than the
Last. Trickles of sweat stretch
Down my spine, tracing each
Rib-like caress, but without ever
Knowing what it feels like to be tickled
By fingerprints.

My roots
Swell and itch waiting for release,
But I don't pull on the sensation
Long enough to make my nose drip
Into the cold winter waste.

Gross and grok is my wame,
Full of lies, despise that follows
My feet like a shadow before exorcism.

How I wish to be pressed like a flower,

Dripping excess scent and honey;
Paper thin, my frame torn
By the slightest movement.

Darkness Hiding

Down the dusk hallway
 The damp walls haunt
 Any new memories that creep through
 Pathways filled with cobwebs and are
consumed
 By the vacuum of space that drifts
 Overhead, an orange light casts a warm glow
 Trapping sections of the ground that would
prefer to be dark.
 But in incandescence secrets are exposed
 To those who may not want to listen.
 And when the sconces burn,
 Everything begins to resemble lines
 Rather than circles.
 Why walk by way of the sun when hiding under
the shade of the moon is safe?

Silver

A whisper caught by silver
Mist swirling over waves
About to break. Before
Crests resemble clouds I run
With river sounds; a cry
For peace, a departure
Into stillness. An echo from
The past pushes
My limit nonetheless.

Balcony

The king smiles from the wall
Next to a familiar old man
That has since dissolved.

The king hasn't been here,
But he's here.

The entrancing, sweet repellent
Of tobacco permeates the furniture, but
They only smoke on the porch.

In the kitchen with two refrigerators,
Ma'amoul rests on the counter where an
Old woman once kneaded dough
And wore light pink slippers.

Floating toward the bedroom
Avoiding the narrow walls,
Slick, with beads dripping down limbs.

The wooden door at the end of the hallway
creaks open.
Twins wearing cross-stitched bed skirts
Stare out at the balcony.

Pushing the glass out,
Climbing onto the platform, careful
Not to fall over the less-than-code railing.

Eyes reflect lights illuminating,
Cobblestone walkways weaving
Through dusk buildings and
Drying bedding on a rack.

Wracked with sobs flowing,
Like the waters through the town below.
Never pausing to allow the concealment
Of moisture wicked with trembling fingers.

Contemplating the necrotic nature of existence.

Longing

Choking on my heart
Feeling the pulse in
The pit of my

Stomach, burning
I whispered softly
Could you help

Me, remember
Where we stand
Across from each other

I turn around
Holding my hair
And you hold your

Breath, I feel on my back
As my own catches
My head creates

Stories, I want you
To be part of
But do you

Want to zip my dress?

There's no choice,
Your hands shake

Fiddling with the
Zipper, zipping my lips
For fear I'd say something
We would both
Regret, but you
Manage, and my

Dress is zipped,
So I turn around
And smile at

You, who I want
More than anything
But I'll never

Say, do you want
To get going?
We'll be late for class

From Flowers

Velvet curtains spiral down posts to hide the
light
 Seeping in from manufacturing errors. The oil
 Coats our throats as we laugh
 In a room void of color.
 But as our humor floats toward the ceiling,
 Opaque petals rain down.

In the vase on the windowsill,
 Swirling water beads haunt the stems of
 Flowers torn from the wild outside.

As we sink down into pillows pushed
 Against walls, we reach for the vase,
 Lifting to our lips the oil of velvet.
 Separating the rain
 From our veins,

Slowly,
 We arrive at a time where no one remembers
 Their name, and it renders us fit to
 Dream in this dark room.

This womb, warm and wasting
 Only has so much more to give.

The oil is ru n n i n g out.

Returning to the windowsill,
We press the petals and once again
Feel on our tongues the
Oiled velvet that
Eclipses our senses and
Threatens our sanity.

Lustrous Moments

Snapping are the whisps of the willow trees,
 Spinning, whirling. Flicking my
 Face as I pass through them, ghost-like, my feet
floating.
 Eyes widening to take in the waterfall,
 Before me, the clear, cool, pool of water
sparkles pink, then purple,
 An array of crystals rolling at the surface,
plunging
 Below to dance with the silver slivers of fish,
scales a shining
 Iridescence. Projections of wings encircle the
scene, white
 And light, cascading through the lapses in
leaves overhead providing
 Warmth. My skin thanks the sun rays,
 For the chill of the glade surprises my body,
conjuring a
 Ripple of flesh strong enough to rival the tide of
the pond,
 Drawing me to it, then pushing me away,
leaving in its
 Wake, swollen trails of saturated sand that
 Caress my feet, then fade as I
 Drift back toward the tree line,

Casting one last glance over my shoulder,
Knowing I will return someday.

Lover

In that garden where our hands first met,
  Where our feet first danced
  And our eyes first spoke.

  I remember when I walked down the busy street
  Taking that slight right turn past the sprawling
vines
  That snaked up each lamp post.
  The cold metal gate separating cigarette smoke
  From the envelope of jasmine perfume.

  Once engulfed I waited for you.
  Standing there with my hair done-up
  And magenta dress that touched mid-thigh.

  You appeared from the tree whose leaves
sprinkled us
  With sunlight from above in houndstooth
  Matching your tie, a shade of grey
  As orphic as your eyes.

Our palms met locking our fingers
In a yearning we could not escape.
Yet we could vanish, together.
Into the fog we stepped,

Our souls aligned.

Left behind were remnants of our
Beating hearts, a single eyelash strewn on the
Bench under the tree from where you first
appeared.

The garden sits empty, awaiting the arrival of
New lovers seeking departure.